UNLEASHING YOUR POTENTIAL

TABLE OF CONTENTS

INTRODUCTION
UNDERSTANDING YOUR POTENTIAL

Welcome to the beginning of a transformative journey—a journey toward realizing your true potential, breaking free from the confines of your current limitations, and stepping into a realm of endless possibilities. The very fact that you're here, ready to embark on this path, is a testament to the latent power within you, eager to unfold. This book is designed to be your guide, your companion, and your catalyst for change as you navigate the intricacies of personal growth and self-improvement.

The Concept of Potential and Its Importance

Potential is a vast, often untapped reservoir of capabilities, talents, and strengths that lie dormant within each of us. It's the difference between where you are now and where you could be, between what you're doing and what you're capable of achieving. Understanding and unlocking your potential is crucial because it is the foundation upon which you can build a life that is not only successful by conventional standards but also deeply fulfilling and meaningful.

Your potential is your gateway to:

- Achieving goals that seem out of reach
- Overcoming obstacles that appear insurmountable
- Developing skills and talents that lie dormant
- Leading a life that aligns with your deepest values and aspirations

In essence, unlocking your potential is about becoming the best version of yourself, not in a comparative sense but in a deeply personal and individual sense. It's about realizing your unique talents and using them to make a positive impact in your world.

Common Myths About Self-Improvement and Personal Growth
As we embark on this journey together, it's essential to dispel some common myths that often hinder our progress toward self-improvement:

- **Myth: There's a Magic Formula for Success**
- Reality: Success and personal growth are highly individualized and require a tailored approach. What works for one person may not work for another. The key is to find what works for you, through trial and reflection.
- **Myth: Change Happens Overnight**
- Reality: Meaningful change is a process, not an event. It involves consistent effort, patience, and resilience. Celebrate small victories along the way, as they are the stepping stones to significant achievements.
- **Myth: You Need to Be Born With Certain Qualities to Succeed**
- Reality: While innate talents can give you a head start, most skills and qualities can be developed through dedication and practice. Growth mindset, resilience, and perseverance are often more critical to success than any innate talent.
- **Myth: Failure Is a Step Backward**
- Reality: Failure is an integral part of the learning process. It provides valuable insights, helping us refine our approach and grow. Embracing failure as a stepping stone rather than a setback is crucial for personal development.

As we move forward, keep an open mind, be willing to challenge your existing beliefs, and prepare to embark on a rewarding journey of self-discovery and growth. Unlocking your potential is not just about reaching a destination; it's about the journey itself—the experiences you'll have, the lessons you'll learn, and the person you'll become along the way.

Welcome to the start of this path of discovery. Together, we will venture in search of our untapped abilities and begin a journey of personal growth and transformation.

CHAPTER 1
THE MINDSET OF GROWTH

Cultivating a Growth Mindset

Beginning a journey of personal transformation and reaching your utmost potential starts with the essential step of developing a mindset focused on growth. This idea embodies a thought process that deeply influences our approach to facing challenges, learning new things, and evolving personally. Unlike a fixed mindset, which perceives abilities and intelligence as static and unchangeable, a growth mindset thrives on challenge and sees failure not as evidence of unintelligence but as a heartening springboard for growth and for stretching our existing abilities.

At the heart of the growth mindset is the belief that skills and intelligence can be developed through dedication, hard work, and persistence. This belief leads to a love of learning and a resilience that is essential for great accomplishment. Here's how you can cultivate a growth mindset and set the stage for unleashing your potential:

Embrace Challenges

Challenges are opportunities for growth. While a fixed mindset might lead you to avoid challenges for fear of failure, a growth mindset encourages you to embrace them. Each challenge is a chance to learn something new and to expand your abilities. Instead of asking, "What if I fail?" ask, "What will I learn?"

Persist in the Face of Setbacks

Setbacks are not indicators of your inability but are part of the learning process. A growth mindset allows you to see setbacks as temporary and surmountable. It encourages you to persist, even when progress seems slow. Remember, resilience is built in the moments when you feel like giving up but choose to keep going.

See Effort as the Path to Mastery

Effort is not something to be avoided with a growth mindset. Instead, it's seen as a necessary part of the journey toward mastery and achievement. Embrace hard work, understanding that effort fosters talent and skills. Celebrate your dedication to growth rather than just the outcomes of your efforts.

Learn from Criticism

Feedback, even when it's critical, is a valuable source of learning. A growth mindset allows you to filter and apply constructive criticism without letting it damage your self-esteem. It means being open to feedback and willing to use it to improve. Instead of defending your ego, focus on how the feedback can help you grow.

Find Lessons and Inspiration in the Success of Others

Instead of feeling threatened by others' success, use it as motivation to learn and grow. A growth mindset encourages you to look for lessons in the achievements of others and to see their successes as inspiration for what's possible.

Cultivating a growth mindset is not about denying your limitations but about embracing the belief that you can overcome them through persistence and effort. It's a commitment to continuous learning and improvement, even in the face of challenges and failures. This mindset is the bedrock upon which you can build your journey toward unlocking your full potential.

As you move forward, remember that cultivating a growth mindset is a practice. It requires mindfulness and the willingness to confront your fixed mindset tendencies. Celebrate your growth, learn from your experiences, and keep pushing the boundaries of what you believe is possible. With a growth mindset, there are no limits to what you can achieve.

Overcoming Limiting Beliefs

Limiting beliefs are those often unconscious beliefs we hold about ourselves and the world that restrict our potential and hold us back from achieving our goals. These beliefs can stem from past experiences, societal messages, or the influence of those around us. They act as barriers to our growth, telling us what we can or cannot do, often without any real basis in fact. Overcoming these limiting beliefs is crucial for cultivating a growth mindset and unlocking our true potential.

Here are strategies to identify and overcome your limiting beliefs:

Identify Your Limiting Beliefs

The first step in overcoming limiting beliefs is to identify them. This process involves self-reflection and honesty. Pay attention to your inner dialogue, especially when facing challenges or setbacks. What are you telling yourself? Are these thoughts empowering or do they hold you back? Common limiting beliefs include thoughts like "I'm not good enough," "I'll never be able to do this," or "I don't deserve success."

Challenge and Question Your Beliefs

Once you've identified a limiting belief, challenge it. Ask yourself, "Is this really true?" "What evidence do I have to support this belief?" and "Are there instances where this belief has not held true?" By questioning the validity of your beliefs, you can start to break down their power over you. Often, you'll find that these beliefs are based on outdated or incorrect assumptions.

Replace Limiting Beliefs with Empowering Beliefs

For every limiting belief, try to formulate an empowering belief that supports your growth and potential. Instead of thinking, "I'm not good enough," you might choose to believe, "I am capable of learning and growing." This process is not about denying your feelings or experiences but about choosing to focus on beliefs that empower you to take action and grow.

Use Positive Affirmations

Positive affirmations can help reinforce your new, empowering beliefs. These are positive statements that you repeat to yourself, designed to challenge negative thoughts and beliefs and replace them with positive ones. For example, "Every day, in every way, I am getting better and better." Make sure your affirmations are in the present tense, positive, and specific.

Take Small Steps
Overcoming limiting beliefs is a process that requires time and patience. Start by taking small steps that challenge these beliefs. If you believe you're not a good public speaker, for example, start by speaking up more in meetings or join a local speaking club. Each small success will build your confidence and reinforce your new, empowering beliefs.

Reflect on Past Successes
When you find yourself doubting your abilities, reflect on your past successes. Remember times when you overcame obstacles or achieved something you were proud of. This reflection can help remind you of your capabilities and resilience, challenging the validity of any limiting beliefs that suggest otherwise.

Seek Support
Sometimes, the best way to overcome limiting beliefs is with the help of others. This could be through a mentor, coach, therapist, or supportive friends and family. These individuals can offer perspective, challenge your limiting beliefs, and support you in your journey towards growth.

Practice Self-Compassion
Finally, be kind to yourself. Overcoming limiting beliefs is challenging work, and it's essential to practice self-compassion along the way. Understand that growth takes time, and it's okay to make mistakes. Treat yourself with the same kindness and understanding you would offer a good friend.

Overcoming limiting beliefs is a crucial step in cultivating a growth mindset and unlocking your potential. By identifying, challenging, and replacing these beliefs with empowering ones, you set the foundation for a life of growth, achievement, and fulfillment.

CHAPTER 2
SETTING AND ACHIEVING GOALS

Setting goals is a fundamental step in unlocking your potential and propelling yourself towards success. In this chapter, we'll explore not only how to set effective goals but also how to break them down into actionable steps that make achievement feasible and measurable.

Effective Goal-Setting Strategies

To effectively set goals, it is essential to structure them in a way that maximizes your potential for success. Here's a comprehensive guide to crafting goals that not only challenge you but also align closely with your personal and professional aspirations:

1. Utilize the SMART Framework: This time-tested method ensures your goals are clear and reachable. Each goal should adhere to the following criteria:
- **Specific**: Define your objectives as precisely as possible. Clear goals provide direction and make it easier to plan the necessary actions.
- **Measurable**: Establish criteria for measuring progress towards the achievement of each goal. This will help you stay on track and recognize when you have succeeded.
- **Achievable**: Your goals should stretch your abilities but remain achievable. Consider your current resources and constraints to ensure realistic planning.
- **Relevant**: Choose goals that matter to you and are aligned with your broader life goals and professional aspirations.

Relevance increases personal commitment and motivation.
- **Time-bound**: Set a specific timeline for achieving your goals. Deadlines help you organize your tasks more effectively and prioritize your efforts.

2. Align Your Goals with Your Values: Make sure your goals resonate with your core personal values. When your goals reflect what is most important to you, they become more meaningful and fulfilling, which naturally enhances your motivation to pursue them.

3. Document Your Goals: Writing down your goals not only commits them to memory but also acts as a persistent reminder of what you aim to achieve. Keeping a dedicated goal journal can also help you monitor your progress and reflect on the adjustments needed as you advance.

4. Share Your Goals: Discussing your goals with a trusted friend, mentor, or coach can significantly enhance your accountability. This support network can provide encouragement and invaluable feedback, helping you refine your approach and overcome obstacles.

5. Regular Review and Adjustment: Because life is inherently dynamic, your goals may need to adapt in response to changing circumstances or new insights. Regularly revisiting and refining your goals ensures they remain relevant and challenging, keeping you engaged and focused on continuous improvement.

6. Expand Your Vision: Beyond immediate or short-term goals, consider setting some long-range goals that challenge the boundaries of your current capabilities and envision a broader future. These visionary goals can inspire deeper passion and drive more profound life transformations.

7. **Create an Action Plan:** Each goal should have a corresponding action plan that outlines the steps necessary to achieve it. This plan should include specific actions, resources required, and intermediate milestones for tracking progress.

By integrating these strategies, you will not only enhance your ability to set effective goals but also increase your overall effectiveness in achieving them. This structured approach to goal setting encourages a disciplined yet flexible methodology that adapts to your personal growth and evolving ambitions, ensuring that each goal you set is a step toward significant personal and professional achievements.

Breaking Down Goals into Actionable Steps

Breaking down your goals into actionable steps is crucial for transforming your aspirations into tangible outcomes. This structured approach not only keeps you organized and motivated but also significantly enhances your ability to achieve what you set out to do. Here's how to meticulously plan and execute this strategy:

1. **Visualize the Outcome:** Start with envisioning the successful realization of your goal. What does the final outcome look like, and how does achieving it make you feel? Visualizing success helps cement your commitment and clarifies the steps needed to get there.

2. **Set Clear Milestones:** Break your main goal into distinct, measurable milestones. Each should represent a significant phase in your journey, marking progress clearly. For example, if your aim is to enhance your professional skills, milestones might include completing specific training courses or obtaining certifications.

3. **Detail Small Tasks:** For each milestone, list out smaller tasks that are necessary to achieve it. These tasks should

be specific enough to act as clear steps towards each milestone. For instance, if a milestone is to learn a new software, tasks could involve scheduling time to practice, completing tutorials, or passing a certification test.

4. **Prioritize Tasks**: Organize tasks by their priority, taking into consideration their impact on your overall goal and any dependencies between tasks. This helps you allocate your time and resources efficiently.

5. **Assign Deadlines**: Deadlines are crucial for maintaining momentum. Set realistic deadlines for each task to create urgency and encourage steady progress.

6. **Create a Daily Schedule**: Integrate tasks into your daily or weekly schedule. Allocating specific times for each task ensures you make consistent progress and helps establish a routine.

7. **Regular Monitoring and Adjusting**: Keep track of your progress with regular reviews of what you've accomplished and what's pending. Adjust your plans based on what is or isn't working, which can involve re-prioritizing tasks or redefining milestones.

8. **Celebrate Achievements**: Acknowledge the completion of each task and milestone. Celebrating these successes fosters motivation and gives you a sense of accomplishment, which is vital for maintaining long-term commitment to your goals.

9. **Maintain Flexibility**: Stay flexible in your approach, allowing for adjustments based on changes in circumstances, new opportunities, or feedback. This adaptability is key to managing any challenges that may arise during your pursuit.

10. **Reflect on Your Progress**: Regularly reflect on the progress made and lessons learned. This reflection helps you understand what strategies are effective and how you can improve moving forward.

11. **Engage in Continuous Learning**: As you work towards your goals, continuously seek out new knowledge and skills that can enhance your ability to succeed. This might involve reading relevant books, attending workshops, or engaging with professionals in your field.

12. **Seek and Use Feedback**: Regular feedback from trusted colleagues or mentors can provide you with insights and perspectives that refine your approach and enhance your strategies for achieving your goals.

By implementing these comprehensive steps, you systematically reduce the complexity of achieving large goals by converting them into smaller, manageable actions. This method not only increases your chances of success but also makes the process more engaging and less overwhelming.

CHAPTER 3
BUILDING RESILIENCE AND OVERCOMING OBSTACLES

Resilience is the capacity to recover quickly from difficulties; it's what enables us to face challenges head-on, adapt to adversity, and come out stronger on the other side. In the journey of self-improvement and achieving our goals, resilience is not just beneficial; it's essential. This section explores strategies to build resilience and maintain your path forward, even in the face of significant challenges.

Strategies for Resilience in the Face of Challenges

Develop a Growth Mindset
- **Embrace Challenges:** View challenges as necessary components of personal growth. Challenges stimulate us to extend beyond our current abilities and often lead us to discover new skills or refine existing ones.
- **Learn from Mistakes:** Instead of viewing mistakes as failures, see them as part of the learning process. Each mistake provides unique insights into what doesn't work, paving the way to discover what will work.
- **Celebrate Effort:** Focus on the effort rather than the outcome. Praising effort cultivates a mindset that values hard work and perseverance, which are critical to overcoming obstacles.

Maintain a Strong Support Network
- **Seek Quality Relationships:** Prioritize relationships that provide mutual support, trust, and positivity. These

relationships can be sources of strength during tough times.

- **Be Proactive in Networking:** Actively engage with new individuals who can bring different perspectives and experiences to your life. Expanding your network can provide new opportunities and resources when facing challenges.
- **Give Support:** Being a supportive friend or colleague also builds your emotional resilience. The act of giving support can make your social ties stronger and foster a supportive culture around you.

Practice Self-Care
- **Establish a Routine:** Create and maintain a daily routine that includes time for physical activity, relaxation, and sleep. Regularity in these areas can significantly enhance your mental and physical readiness to face life's stresses.
- **Mindfulness Practices:** Incorporate practices such as yoga, meditation, or deep-breathing exercises into your daily routine to enhance mindfulness, which helps reduce stress by focusing your mind on the present moment.
- **Hobbies and Interests:** Engage in hobbies or activities that you enjoy. These can serve as a distraction from stress and recharge your energy and creativity.

Set Realistic Goals
- **Use SMART Goals:** Ensure your goals are Specific, Measurable, Attainable, Relevant, and Time-bound. SMART goals help clarify your focus and provide measurable benchmarks for tracking progress.
- **Adjust as Necessary:** Regularly review and adjust your goals based on your progress and any changes in your situation. This flexibility can help you stay committed to your objectives without feeling overwhelmed.
- **Celebrate Small Wins:** Recognize and celebrate each small victory along the way. This builds confidence and

motivation, which are essential for tackling larger challenges.

Embrace Flexibility
- **Cultivate an Adaptive Mindset:** Develop the ability to adjust quickly to new challenges, setbacks, or information. An adaptive mindset is a cornerstone of resilience.
- **Plan for Various Outcomes:** While maintaining focus on your goals, prepare for different scenarios. Planning for multiple outcomes can reduce the shock and stress of sudden changes.
- **Stay Open to Learning:** View every situation, especially the difficult ones, as an opportunity to learn something new. This openness not only helps you adapt but also grows your knowledge and experience base.

These detailed strategies for building resilience can empower you to face life's challenges more effectively. By developing a growth mindset, maintaining strong relationships, practicing self-care, setting realistic goals, and embracing flexibility, you equip yourself with the tools needed to overcome obstacles and emerge stronger.

Learning from Failure
Failure is an inevitable part of life and a critical element of growth and success. Understanding how to learn from failure is essential for building resilience and ensuring continuous improvement. Here's a deeper look into effective strategies for learning from failure:

Normalize Failure
- **Reframe Failure:** Change your perspective on failure. Instead of seeing it as a negative end result, view it as a vital part of the experimentation process that leads to innovation and discovery.

- **Cultural Acceptance:** Work towards creating an environment, whether at work or in personal life, where failure is seen as a step towards success, not a setback. This acceptance can dramatically reduce the fear of trying new things and encourage more creative and ambitious endeavors.

Analyze and Reflect
- **Detailed Review:** After a setback, conduct a thorough analysis of the events that led to the failure. What were the contributing factors? Were there warning signs? Understanding the specifics can prevent future mistakes.
- **Write It Down:** Documenting your failures and their circumstances can be a useful tool for reflection. Writing provides clarity and can be a reference to track your learning over time.

Extract Lessons
- **Focus on Learnings:** With every failure, actively look for lessons. What can be learned from this experience? How can these learnings be applied to future projects or decisions?
- **Systematic Application:** Once lessons are identified, think about how they can be systematically implemented into future strategies to avoid repeating the same mistakes.

Resilience Feedback Loop
- **Iterative Process:** Treat the process of dealing with failures as iterative. Each loop through failure and reflection should bring improvements. This is the essence of developing resilience.
- **Integrate Feedback:** Integrate the insights gained from each failure into your standard operating procedures or personal habits. This continual integration helps build a robust framework for handling future challenges.

Seek Feedback
- **Consult Peers and Mentors:** Sometimes it's difficult to see our own blind spots. Consulting with peers, mentors, or even a coach can provide new perspectives and valuable insights that you might not have considered.
- **Openness to Critique:** Cultivate a receptiveness to constructive criticism. Seeing feedback as a gift rather than a criticism can change how you respond to and learn from it.

Maintain Persistence
- **Long-Term Vision:** Keep your eyes on your long-term goals and do not be disheartened by temporary setbacks. Persistence is key to overcoming challenges.
- **Emotional Resilience:** Develop your emotional resilience by managing your reactions to failure. Recognize the emotions that come with setbacks, address them healthily, and move forward with renewed focus.

By embracing these strategies, you can transform failure from a feared outcome into a powerful stepping stone towards success. Learning from failure not only enhances your resilience but also equips you with the wisdom to navigate future challenges more effectively.

CHAPTER 4
THE POWER OF HABITS

The Role of Habits in Personal Transformation

Habits play a pivotal role in personal transformation. They are the small, often automatic behaviors that accumulate over time to shape the fabric of our lives. By understanding and modifying our habits, we can exert significant control over our trajectories and ultimately steer our lives in the direction we wish to go.

Foundation of Daily Life: Habits undeniably form the bedrock of our everyday existence, shaping the rhythm and flow of our daily lives in profound ways. From the moment we open our eyes in the morning to the instant we drift off to sleep at night, the habits we've cultivated play a pivotal role in sculpting our actions, interactions, and reactions. These routines, often performed subconsciously, serve as the invisible architects of our day, influencing not just the major milestones but also the minute, seemingly inconsequential moments. Whether it's the ritual of brewing a morning cup of coffee that kickstarts our day, the habitual midday walk that clears our mind and re-energizes our spirit, or the nightly routine of reflecting on the day's events that helps us wind down and prepare for rest, these patterns hold sway over much of our behavior. They are the silent conductors orchestrating the symphony of our day-to-day lives, guiding how we start our mornings with intention, how we navigate the complexities of social interactions, and how we find solace and rejuvenation in our nightly routines. In essence, our habits lay the tracks upon which the train of our daily life runs, determining the pace, direction, and quality of our journey.

Catalysts for Change: Deliberately shifting our habits strikes at the heart of the intricate machinery that molds our daily existence. When we embark on the journey to alter these entrenched patterns, we're engaging with the fundamental processes that sculpt our reality. This pursuit is not merely about tweaking minor behaviors; it's about initiating a transformative cascade that can revolutionize our health, amplify our productivity, enrich our relationships, and elevate our overall sense of well-being. A single change in habit, no matter how small it may seem, can act as a powerful lever, capable of lifting us to new heights of personal achievement and satisfaction. It's akin to throwing a pebble into a still pond; the ripples extend far beyond the initial point of impact, affecting every aspect of our lives. Whether it's adopting a more nutritious diet, dedicating time to mindfulness, or prioritizing meaningful connections, each new habit plants the seeds for a richer, more fulfilled existence. In essence, by choosing to modify our habits, we're not just altering our routines; we're reshaping our destiny, one day at a time, turning the ordinary into the extraordinary and transforming the fabric of our daily life into a tapestry woven with the threads of progress and growth.

Efficiency and Automation: Our brains are hardwired to streamline efficiency, crafting habits as a means to conserve energy. When an action evolves into a habit, it transitions into a lower-consciousness state, allowing us to perform it with scant mental engagement. This process is akin to automating a software task on a computer, where the system runs the program in the background, liberating the processor to tackle more complex tasks. This neurological efficiency is a double-edged sword; it serves us exceptionally well when the habit fosters productivity, health, or positivity, essentially automating beneficial behaviors that enhance our lives without demanding constant deliberation or willpower. For instance, the habit of morning exercise or nightly reading becomes a seamless part of our routine, contributing to our well-being while requiring minimal mental bandwidth. However, this same efficiency mechanism can work against us if the habit in question is detrimental. Negative behaviors, once habitual, can persist under the radar of our conscious mind, quietly undermining our health, productivity, and happiness. Thus, while the brain's capacity for habit formation is a marvel of cognitive economy, enabling us to navigate daily life with ease and grace, it also necessitates a mindful approach to which behaviors we allow to become habitual. Recognizing and redirecting harmful habits while cultivating positive ones is essential in harnessing this neural efficiency for our overall benefit, turning the brain's inclination for automation into a powerful tool for personal development and well-being.

The Habit Loop: Embedded within the structure of each habit lies a cyclical process known as the habit loop, a concept critical to deciphering how habits form and endure. This loop is composed of three distinct elements: the cue, which acts as the initial trigger for the behavior; the routine, which is the behavior executed in response to the cue; and the reward, the positive reinforcement that cements the behavior into a habit. The cue ignites an almost automatic reaction, leading to the routine - the action we're inclined to perform. Subsequently, the reward delivers a satisfying payoff, reinforcing the loop and ensuring the cycle's continuation.
Grasping the intricacies of this loop is instrumental in both the development of new, beneficial habits and the alteration of those we wish to discard. By identifying the cues that prompt undesirable behaviors, we can either eliminate these triggers or replace the negative routines they incite with more positive actions, all while ensuring that the reward remains compelling enough to solidify this new behavior. Similarly, when fostering new habits, consciously crafting this loop by selecting specific cues to initiate desirable routines, followed by rewarding outcomes, can effectively embed these practices into our daily lives.

Understanding the habit loop offers a powerful lens through which we can view our behaviors, providing a blueprint for change that lies at the heart of habit formation. It equips us with the knowledge to strategically intervene and reshape our actions, turning the automatic nature of habits from an unconscious force into a deliberate tool for personal growth and improvement.

Small Changes, Big Impact: The principle that minor adjustments to our habits can yield significant, transformative results over time is a testament to the power of the compound effect. This concept, akin to the financial principle of compound interest, suggests that even minimal enhancements or changes in our daily behaviors can accumulate, resulting in substantial long-term benefits. Just as a small amount of money saved or invested can grow exponentially over years, so too can incremental improvements in our habits lead to profound changes in our well-being, productivity, and overall quality of life.

Imagine the impact of dedicating just a few more minutes to reading each day, or the positive shift that can occur from adding a single piece of fruit to your diet regularly. These actions, seemingly insignificant in isolation, can enhance cognitive function, contribute to better health, and foster a lifelong habit of learning and growth when practiced consistently over time.

Moreover, this approach of making small, manageable changes removes the intimidation factor often associated with attempting major life overhauls. It encourages a mindset of continuous improvement, where the journey of personal development is viewed as a series of small steps rather than a single, monumental leap. By focusing on the attainable goal of making just a 1% improvement, individuals can feel more empowered and less overwhelmed, leading to greater consistency and, ultimately, meaningful progress.

The beauty of small changes lies in their ability to generate momentum. As these minor adjustments become ingrained habits, they set the stage for further improvements, creating a virtuous cycle of positive change. This ripple effect can extend beyond the individual, influencing their environment, relationships, and the broader community in unexpectedly positive ways.

In essence, the philosophy of small changes, big impact underscores the notion that the path to achieving our grandest goals and aspirations is paved with the bricks of modest, daily actions. Embracing this principle can not only facilitate personal transformation but also inspire a more intentional and fulfilling approach to life.

Building Positive Habits: Constructing positive habits is akin to laying the foundation for a healthier, more productive, and fulfilling life. This transformative process begins with a clear vision of the outcomes you wish to achieve, whether it's improving your physical health, enhancing your productivity, or fostering a sense of well-being. Understanding the mechanics behind your current behaviors—specifically, the habit loops of cue, routine, and reward—is essential in pinpointing where changes can be most effectively applied.

The journey to cultivating positive habits is one of deliberate and thoughtful modification of these habit loops. It involves identifying the triggers (cues) that lead to certain behaviors (routines) and the satisfaction derived from them (rewards). By dissecting this process, you can begin to replace negative routines with positive ones while maintaining or modifying the cue and ensuring the reward is still fulfilling. For example, if stress triggers a habit of unhealthy snacking (cue and routine), replacing snacking with a brief walk or meditation session (new routine) could provide relaxation and satisfaction (reward) without compromising health.

This method of small, incremental changes is both manageable and sustainable. It allows for gradual improvement without the overwhelm that can accompany attempts to overhaul behavior overnight. Each small change builds upon the last, creating a compounding effect that, over time, results in significant transformation. This approach also encourages experimentation and adaptation, recognizing that not every change will be successful on the first try and that habits can and should evolve with your goals and circumstances.

Moreover, building positive habits is not a solitary endeavor. Seeking support from friends, family, or communities who share similar goals can provide encouragement, accountability, and inspiration. Sharing your successes and challenges not only reinforces your commitment but also contributes to a collective knowledge base that can benefit others on their journey.

In essence, constructing positive habits is a strategic process that involves careful analysis of existing patterns, thoughtful planning of new routines, and a commitment to gradual, consistent improvement. By focusing on the underlying structure of our behaviors and taking small steps toward change, we can effectively shape our habits to support our long-term goals and aspirations, paving the way for a more intentional and rewarding life.

The power of habits lies in their remarkable capacity to fundamentally alter our daily lives and overall trajectory. Through intentionally cultivating and refining our habits, we tap into a potent force for personal evolution and enduring transformation. Recognizing how habits impact our journey towards self-improvement marks the initial leap into harnessing this dynamic energy. It paves the way for us to fully realize our capabilities and sculpt a life that aligns with our deepest aspirations. In embracing this understanding, we set the stage for a profound shift, one that enables us to unlock our utmost potential and embark on a path rich with growth, discovery, and fulfillment.

Creating and maintaining positive habits

Creating and maintaining positive habits is a foundational aspect of achieving personal aspirations and significantly boosting overall well-being. This structured methodology not only facilitates the establishment of beneficial habits but also ensures their sustainability over time, allowing for profound and lasting change. Here's an expanded approach to help you embed these positive routines into your life.

Step 1: Identify and Understand Your Motivation

- **Discover Your 'Why':** Begin by exploring the reasons behind your desire to cultivate a new habit. Whether it's improving your health, enhancing productivity, or fostering a deeper sense of inner peace, understanding the core motivation behind your goal is crucial. This insight serves as the fuel to keep you motivated during challenging times and provides a clear perspective on your progress.
- **Align Habits with Values:** Reflect on how this habit aligns with your values and long-term objectives. Ensuring that your new habit supports broader life goals reinforces the importance of this change, making it more meaningful and sustainable.

Step 2: Break It Down into Manageable Steps

Transforming a broad goal into a set of actionable, daily habits is akin to charting a path through unexplored territory. The journey is made not in leaps but in careful, deliberate steps.

- **Small Steps:** Begin by deconstructing your new habit into its most basic components. If your goal is to read more books, start with something as simple as reading a page a night. These micro-actions might seem trivial at first glance, but they play a crucial role in overcoming inertia and resistance. By minimizing the initial effort required, you're far more likely to get started and, just as importantly, to continue. Integrating these tiny habits into your daily routine becomes almost effortless, setting the foundation for more substantial changes over time.
- **Incremental Progress:** As these small actions start to become a natural part of your daily life, incrementally challenge yourself by gradually increasing the difficulty or duration of the habit. Following the reading example, once a page a night becomes a habit, escalate to a chapter

a night. This method of progressive overload applies not just to physical training but to habit formation of all kinds. It ensures that you're continuously pushing the boundaries of your comfort zone without stepping so far outside it that the habit becomes unsustainable.

This step-by-step progression leverages the principle of compounding, where the effects of small, consistent actions accumulate over time, leading to significant achievements. By focusing on incremental progress, you allow yourself the time and space to adapt to each new level of demand, making the process of habit formation both manageable and rewarding. This approach fosters a sense of accomplishment and confidence with each step forward, reinforcing your commitment to the habit and to your broader goals.

Step 3: Identify Triggers and Rewards

The creation of a new habit or the alteration of an existing one can significantly benefit from understanding and utilizing the cue-routine-reward loop, a concept central to habit formation. This loop begins with a cue, a specific trigger that tells your brain to go into automatic mode and which habit to use. The routine is the behavior itself, which can be physical, mental, or emotional. Following the routine is the reward, which helps your brain figure out if this particular loop is worth remembering for the future.

- **Cue-Routine-Reward:** Start by pinpointing a precise cue for your intended habit. This could be a time of day, a particular location, an emotional state, or the occurrence of a specific event. Next, define the routine, which is the habit you're aiming to cultivate. Finally, identify a reward that directly follows the routine. This reward should be something genuinely appealing to you, creating a positive association with the habit. For instance, if you're trying to make a habit of running in the morning, the cue might be the alarm clock ringing at a specific time, the routine is the run itself, and the reward could be the exhilarating feeling of energy and alertness that follows your exercise.

- **Make It Satisfying:** The reward needs to be immediately gratifying to effectively reinforce the habit. This immediate satisfaction is what tells your brain that the effort of performing the routine is worth it. Rewards can vary greatly depending on the individual and the habit being formed. They might include the intrinsic satisfaction from knowing you're working towards your goal, a piece of chocolate after completing a study session, or a few minutes of downtime after doing a household chore. The key is to ensure the reward is something you truly enjoy and look forward to.

Step 4: Leverage Existing Routines

Building new habits can be made more accessible by anchoring them to routines that are already well-established in your daily life. This technique, known as habit stacking, involves adding your new habit directly before or after a preexisting one, creating a chain of habits.

- **Habit Stacking:** To implement this strategy, first identify a routine already embedded in your daily life. Then, immediately before or after this existing routine, insert the new habit you're trying to develop. For instance, if you wish to cultivate the habit of gratitude journaling and you already have a nightly routine of drinking tea before bed, you could stack your new habit on top of this by journaling while you enjoy your tea. The existing routine serves as a natural cue for the new habit, seamlessly integrating it into your daily life.

By methodically identifying triggers and rewards and skillfully leveraging existing routines, you create a robust framework that supports the development and maintenance of new habits. These strategies not only make the habit formation process more structured but also more intuitive, enhancing the likelihood of long-term success.

Step 5: Create a Supportive Environment

The environment in which we operate can significantly influence our behavior, making it either easier or more challenging to adopt new habits. By consciously designing an environment that supports your goals, you can lower the barriers to performing your new habit and increase your chances of success.

- **Remove Obstacles:** Begin by identifying and eliminating any barriers that make it difficult to practice your new habit. If you're trying to eat healthier, for instance, clear out junk food from your pantry. If you want to start jogging in the morning, prepare your running clothes and shoes the night before. By removing these obstacles, you reduce the friction associated with starting the habit, making it more likely that you'll stick with it.

- **Cultivate Positive Cues:** Just as important as removing obstacles is the addition of positive cues to your environment that prompt your new habit. These can be visual reminders, such as post-it notes on the bathroom mirror reminding you to floss or a water bottle on your desk prompting you to stay hydrated. The key is to make these cues prominent in your environment so they catch your attention and trigger the desired behavior.

Step 6: Track Your Progress

Monitoring your progress is crucial for maintaining motivation and assessing the effectiveness of your habit formation efforts. It provides concrete evidence of your achievements and helps keep you accountable.

- **Use a Habit Tracker:** There are many tools available for tracking habits, from simple pen-and-paper methods to sophisticated mobile apps. Choose a tracking method that you find easy and enjoyable to use. Consistently logging your daily progress helps to maintain your focus and provides a visual representation of your commitment and achievements.

- **Celebrate Milestones:** Setting and recognizing milestones within your habit formation journey can significantly boost your motivation. Whether it's sticking to your new habit for a week, a month, or any other significant period, take the time to celebrate these achievements. Small rewards or celebrations can serve as a form of positive reinforcement, making the habit more rewarding to maintain.

Step 7: Stay Flexible and Patient

Flexibility and patience are vital qualities in the habit formation process. Not every strategy will work perfectly from the start, and adjustments may be necessary as you learn more about what works best for you.

- **Be Willing to Adjust:** If you find that a particular cue, routine, or reward isn't working as well as you hoped, don't hesitate to tweak your approach. The goal is to find the most effective strategy for you, which may require some experimentation.
- **Cultivate Patience:** Habits take time to form, and expecting immediate perfection can lead to frustration. Remind yourself that progress, not perfection, is the goal. Be patient with yourself and recognize that setbacks are part of the learning process. With time and persistence, the new habit will become a natural part of your routine.

By carefully shaping your environment, diligently tracking your progress, and maintaining flexibility and patience, you significantly increase your chances of successfully integrating new, positive habits into your life. These steps provide a comprehensive approach to habit formation, paving the way for lasting personal growth and improvement.

Step 8: Reflection and Continuous Adaptation

This final step emphasizes the importance of continual assessment and adaptation of your habits to ensure they remain relevant and effective as your circumstances and goals evolve.

- **Regular Reflection:** Set aside regular time to reflect on the habits you have developed. Assess whether these habits are still serving their original purpose or need to be adjusted. Reflection can occur through personal journals, discussions with a coach, or simply moments of meditation.
- **Adapt Habits:** Based on your reflections, be prepared to adapt or modify your habits. If a particular habit no longer provides the desired benefits or has proven less effective in your current life context, consider adjusting it or replacing it with something more suitable.
- **Continuous Experimentation:** Maintain an openness to experimentation. Try new techniques or approaches to improve or replace existing habits. Experimentation can lead to significant discoveries about what works best for you.

By implementing this step, you ensure that the habit formation process remains dynamic and personally relevant. Reflection and continuous adaptation allow you to better respond to life's changing challenges and maximize the benefits of your habits in the long term.

Creating and maintaining positive habits is truly a dynamic and evolving journey that unfolds through clear goal-setting, strategic planning, unwavering commitment, and ongoing adaptation. By embracing this structured yet flexible approach, you are well-equipped to integrate new, beneficial habits into the fabric of your daily life, paving the way for profound personal growth and continual enhancement. It's crucial to understand that personal transformation begins with a single habit—a singular change that initiates a cascade of positive developments. As you progress on this path, remember that each step forward, each adjustment made, and each reflection considered, is an integral part of a broader journey toward realizing your fullest potential.

CHAPTER 5
EMOTIONAL INTELLIGENCE AND RELATIONSHIPS

Developing Emotional Intelligence

Emotional Intelligence (EI) represents an essential set of cognitive abilities that enables one to recognize, understand, manage, and reason with emotions, both within oneself and in others. Cultivating EI is integral not just for personal contentment and growth but also for fostering healthy and sustainable relationships in all spheres of life. Here's a deep dive into enhancing your emotional intelligence:

1. Self-awareness
- **Identify Your Emotions:** Cultivating self-awareness begins with the ability to accurately identify and name your emotions as they arise. It's not just about broad feelings such as happiness or anger but also about more nuanced emotions like disappointment, frustration, or contentment. To enhance this awareness, practice mindfulness and tune into your body's signals. For instance, an accelerated heartbeat could indicate anxiety, while a sensation of tightness in your chest might signal stress or apprehension. Acknowledging these physical sensations can help you connect with your emotional state.
- **Monitor Emotional Reactions:** Notice how your emotions influence your thoughts and behaviors. Do certain situations consistently evoke strong emotional reactions? Understanding these patterns can provide valuable insights into your personality.

- **Keep an Emotion Journal:** Documenting your emotional experiences can serve as a powerful tool for increasing self-awareness. Record not only your feelings but also the circumstances that led to these emotions. Over time, you'll be able to detect patterns in your emotional responses and identify triggers. This journal serves as a reflective space where you can contemplate your emotions in depth, understand their origins, and consider healthier ways to manage them.

2. Self-regulation

- **Practice Self-control:** Developing self-control is a key aspect of self-regulation and involves managing disruptive emotions and impulses effectively. It's not about suppression but rather about recognizing your feelings and choosing how you'll react to them. Techniques such as deep breathing can be instrumental in this process, as they help calm the nervous system and provide space between feeling and action. Deep breathing can be practiced almost anywhere and anytime, serving as an anchor in moments of emotional turbulence.
- **Mindfulness Meditation:** Engaging in mindfulness meditation regularly can also enhance your self-regulation. It involves observing your thoughts and emotions without judgment, which can improve your ability to manage them without becoming overwhelmed or reactive.
- **Cognitive Reframing:** This involves consciously shifting your perspective on a situation to view it in a more positive or neutral light. By changing your thoughts, you can change your emotional response, leading to more controlled actions.
- **Set Clear Boundaries:** Establishing clear boundaries is an essential part of emotional self-regulation. Boundaries help you define what you are comfortable with and how you expect to be treated by others. By knowing and asserting these limits, you are more likely to maintain self-

control in situations that might otherwise be emotionally charged.

- **Communicate Boundaries:** It's not enough to know your boundaries; you must also feel confident in communicating them to others. This may involve assertiveness training, where you learn to express your needs and concerns clearly and respectfully without infringing on the rights of others.
- **Recognize Trigger Situations:** Be aware of situations, people, or environments that challenge your emotional regulation. By understanding these triggers, you can either avoid them or prepare strategies in advance to deal with them more effectively.
- **Prioritize Self-Care:** Regularly engaging in self-care activities can strengthen your emotional resilience, making it easier to practice self-regulation. This could include physical activity, pursuing hobbies, or ensuring you have enough rest.

By strengthening your self-regulation through these techniques, you empower yourself to maintain composure, make thoughtful decisions, and respond to situations and challenges in a way that aligns with your values and goals. Self-regulation is not about perfection but progress, and with practice, you can improve your ability to manage your emotions constructively.

3. Motivation

- **Set Personal Goals:** Utilizing your emotional intelligence to pinpoint and articulate your deepest aspirations is a fundamental step in kindling motivation. Goals that resonate with your core values carry an intrinsic power that can propel you forward. Begin by introspecting on what brings you genuine satisfaction, joy, and a sense of purpose. Craft goals that not only challenge and stretch your capabilities but also reflect who you are and what you believe in. When your goals are deeply rooted in your personal values, the drive to achieve them becomes part of your identity, fueling perseverance and dedication.

- **Visualize Success:** Empower your goal-setting by visualizing the successful achievement of your goals. Visualization is a potent technique that involves creating a detailed mental image of the desired outcome. This practice can enhance motivation and increase confidence in your ability to reach your goals, as it pre-conditions the brain to recognize and pursue the path to success.
- **Break Down Large Goals:** Large, long-term goals can sometimes feel daunting. Break them into smaller, manageable tasks that act as stepping stones toward the ultimate goal. This not only makes the process more manageable but also allows for frequent moments of achievement, which can boost motivation.
- **Stay Positive:** Maintaining a positive mindset is key to sustaining motivation, especially when faced with setbacks or challenges. Adopt an optimistic yet realistic outlook that focuses on positive outcomes, viewing obstacles not as impenetrable barriers but as opportunities to learn and grow. This doesn't mean ignoring difficulties; instead, it's about approaching them with the attitude that they are part of the journey and not the end of the road.
- **Reframe Setbacks:** When confronted with setbacks, use your emotional intelligence to reframe these experiences. Instead of interpreting them as failures, view them as valuable feedback and learning opportunities. Analyze what didn't work and why, and use these insights to adjust your strategies and approaches moving forward.
- **Celebrate Progress:** Acknowledge and celebrate the progress you make towards your goals, no matter how small. Recognizing your own efforts and achievements serves as an affirmation of your abilities and reinforces your commitment to your goals.
- **Stay Connected to Your Why:** Regularly remind yourself of the reasons behind your goals. When your actions are

anchored to a meaningful purpose, your motivation to persist and succeed is significantly bolstered.

Cultivating motivation through emotional intelligence involves a conscious commitment to aligning your goals with your deepest values, maintaining a positive perspective, and viewing setbacks as growth opportunities. This strategic approach to fostering motivation ensures a resilient drive that persists in the face of life's inevitable ebbs and flows.

4. Empathy

Empathy is the emotional compass that allows us to navigate the feelings of others, enabling a deep connection and understanding that transcends mere verbal communication.

- **Practice Active Listening:** To fully comprehend another person's perspective, active listening is essential. This involves engaging with the speaker both verbally and non-verbally. Giving someone your undivided attention signifies that you value their words and emotions. Eye contact plays a crucial role in this process, conveying your focus and concern. Meanwhile, body language, such as nodding and leaning forward, can further demonstrate your engagement.
- **Acknowledge Feelings:** As you listen, it's important to recognize and validate the speaker's feelings. This can be done through verbal affirmations or appropriate emotional responses. For instance, saying "That sounds really challenging" when someone shares a difficulty or a simple "I can see why you're excited" when they share good news. Such responses not only affirm the other person's feelings but also build trust, showing that you are truly attuned to their emotional state.
- **Reflect on the Content:** Take moments within the conversation to summarize or paraphrase what the speaker has said. This ensures that you understand their message correctly and gives them the opportunity to clarify if necessary. It also shows that you're not just

hearing, but also processing and deeply understanding their message.

- **Ask Empathetic Questions:** To deepen your understanding and show genuine interest, ask questions that encourage the speaker to elaborate on their feelings and experiences. Questions like "How did that make you feel?" or "What was going through your mind when that happened?" can prompt further sharing and show that you're invested in getting to know their emotional journey.
- **Avoid Immediate Judgment or Advice:** While it may be tempting to offer advice or assess the situation from your perspective, it's important to refrain from doing so right away. Empathetic listening is about allowing the other person to be heard and understood without the pressure of being evaluated or fixed.

Empathy in action is more than a skill—it's a demonstration of our shared humanity and a bridge to deeper, more meaningful relationships. By practicing empathy with intentionality, we not only foster connections with others but also enrich our own emotional experiences, allowing us to grow in understanding and compassion.

5. Social Skills

Social skills are the tools we use to interact and communicate with others effectively. They are crucial for building and maintaining personal and professional relationships.

- **Improve Communication:** Clear communication is about expressing your thoughts and emotions in a way that is easy for others to understand, and doing so with respect and consideration for their perspectives. To enhance your communication skills, focus on being concise and direct while also being mindful of your tone and body language. Avoid using jargon or ambiguous language that could lead to misunderstandings. Instead, choose words that are specific and accurate to your meaning. Reflect on how your words might be received by considering the listener's viewpoint. This respectful approach to expression is instrumental in fostering trust and openness in your relationships.

- **Engage in Active Dialogue:** Effective communication is a two-way street. Encourage dialogue by asking open-ended questions and showing interest in the responses. This invites a deeper exchange of ideas and shows that you value the other person's input.

- **Develop Conflict Resolution Skills:** Conflict is a natural part of human interaction, but it doesn't have to be destructive. To resolve conflicts constructively, approach each situation with a mindset geared towards finding a resolution that acknowledges and addresses the needs and feelings of all parties involved. Start by clearly defining the issue at hand without personalizing the problem. Use "I" statements to express how the conflict affects you, and listen actively when others share their perspectives. Look for common ground or areas of mutual interest as a basis for a solution.

- **Learn Negotiation Techniques:** Conflict resolution often requires negotiation skills. Prepare for discussions by understanding both your needs and those of the other person. Aim for solutions that offer mutual benefits, where compromise doesn't mean loss, but rather a cooperative step towards a shared goal.

- **Practice Empathy:** In both communication and conflict resolution, empathy is key. It allows you to understand and consider others' emotions, leading to more effective and compassionate interaction.

Social skills like effective communication and conflict resolution are essential for navigating the complex dynamics of our interactions with others. These skills enable us to build relationships based on mutual respect and understanding, which are essential for both personal fulfillment and professional success. By continually practicing and refining these skills, we can improve our ability to connect with others and enhance the quality of our social interactions.

Enhancing relationships through the cultivation of emotional intelligence (EI) is a powerful strategy that can lead to more profound connections and interactions.

Understand and Meet Emotional Needs: Recognizing and addressing emotional needs is pivotal. It involves tuning into your own feelings as well as those of others to create a supportive and nurturing environment. When people feel emotionally understood and supported, relationships can deepen and become more fulfilling. It is about creating a space where emotions are not only recognized but also valued and met with appropriate responses. Whether providing comfort during distress or sharing joy in moments of happiness, meeting emotional needs is a testament to a truly empathetic and connected relationship.

Build Trust and Respect: Trust and respect are the bedrock of any strong relationship, and EI is essential in fostering both. Trust is cultivated through consistent and honest communication, following through on commitments, and showing reliability in your actions. Respect is garnered not just by listening to what others have to say but also by valuing their opinions and treating them with dignity, regardless of the situation. When you demonstrate a high level of emotional intelligence, such as the ability to manage your emotions and understand those of others, it lays a foundation of trust and respect that is unshakeable.

Navigate Social Situations: High EI is an invaluable tool in a broad array of social contexts. With heightened emotional intelligence, you have the sensitivity to read a room, the adaptability to mold to various social dynamics, and the skills to communicate effectively. In casual gatherings, this might mean bringing warmth and inclusivity to your interactions, whereas, in more formal or complex situations like negotiations, it can translate into strategic empathy and the ability to build rapport. High EI enables you to approach each social scenario with a nuanced understanding, ensuring that you can connect authentically and navigate interactions with poise and insight.

The development of EI is a transformative process, enhancing not only personal relationships but also professional ones. It invites a level of depth and understanding that enriches interactions, making them more rewarding and effective. With each step taken to enhance your EI, you are not only investing in your own growth but also contributing to healthier, more resilient relationships.

Improving personal and professional relationships

Improving personal and professional relationships is a comprehensive endeavor that demands deliberate effort, nuanced understanding, and ongoing refinement. Applying emotional intelligence and honing interpersonal skills are crucial for deepening the connections you share with those around you. Here's a broader perspective on how to cultivate relationships that are not only healthy but also rewarding and fulfilling, both personally and professionally:

1. Practice Active Listening

- **Engage Fully:** When listening, dedicate your entire focus to the speaker. Turn off distractions, both physical (like your phone) and mental (like your inner dialogue), to truly engage with what's being communicated. This level of engagement shows profound respect for the speaker and signifies that their thoughts and feelings are worthy of your undivided attention.
- **Reflect and Clarify:** Active listening also involves reflecting on what you've heard and asking questions that encourage the speaker to expand on their thoughts. By summarizing their points and seeking clarity, you not only ensure you've understood their message accurately but also validate their feelings, promoting a deeper level of discourse.

2. Express Empathy

- **Understand Emotions:** Make a concerted effort to grasp the emotions underlying the words and actions of others. This deep dive into empathy allows you to forge emotional connections that are the bedrock of trust and rapport in any relationship.
- **Respond with Compassion:** Responding to others with compassion means acknowledging their feelings genuinely and offering your support. Such a response creates an environment of emotional safety, where individuals feel seen, heard, and valued.

3. Communicate Clearly and Constructively

- **Be Direct and Honest:** Communicate your inner world with clarity and respect. This transparency is the foundation of trust and can prevent many misunderstandings that arise from unclear or dishonest communication.
- **Use "I" Statements:** Communicate your perspective using "I" statements to articulate your feelings and needs without casting blame. This approach fosters a constructive dialogue and encourages a reciprocal openness.

4. Set and Respect Boundaries

- **Define Personal Boundaries:** Articulating your personal boundaries with clarity and respect safeguards your well-being and sets the tone for how you expect to be treated.
- **Honor Others' Boundaries:** Show your respect for others by acknowledging and honoring the boundaries they set. This mutual understanding is key to maintaining healthy and respectful relationships.

5. Manage Conflicts Effectively

- **Approach with a Problem-solving Attitude:** Treat conflicts as chances to enhance your relationship through collaborative problem-solving, rather than as roadblocks.

- **Seek Win-win Solutions:** Strive for resolutions that address the needs of all parties involved. This cooperative approach strengthens partnerships and promotes collective success.

6. Show Appreciation and Gratitude
- **Express Gratitude:** Make it a habit to recognize and express appreciation for what others bring into your life. Gratitude is a powerful positive force that can reinforce bonds and encourage more positive interactions.
- **Celebrate Achievements:** Actively celebrate the accomplishments of those around you. Acknowledging both personal and professional successes fosters a shared joy and enhances communal bonds.

7. Invest Time and Effort
- **Prioritize Relationships:** Consciously allocate time and effort to nurture your relationships. The investment of quality time is indispensable for deepening connections.
- **Be Present:** Ensure that when you are with someone, you are fully there, both physically and mentally. Your presence is a testament to how much you value the relationship.

8. Cultivate Self-awareness and Self-improvement
- **Reflect on Your Role:** Engage in regular reflection on how you contribute to each relationship. This self-awareness can reveal areas for improvement and growth.
- **Pursue Personal Growth:** Continuous self-improvement, especially in areas of emotional intelligence and communication, can have a ripple effect on the quality of your relationships.

Improving relationships is an evolving process that has a profound impact on your happiness, well-being, and success. By integrating these strategies thoughtfully and consistently, you can forge stronger and more significant connections. The relationships we cultivate can substantially color our experiences, and thus, investing in them with intent and dedication can lead to a richer, more fulfilling life.

CHAPTER 6
MANAGING STRESS AND ANXIETY

In the whirlwind of modern life, stress and anxiety have emerged as ubiquitous challenges, with pervasive effects on our physical health, mental clarity, and the richness of our daily experiences. Developing a toolkit for managing these states is not just beneficial but essential for fostering resilience and sustaining our well-being. Below are expanded techniques and insights into navigating stress and anxiety effectively:

Techniques for Managing Stress and Anxiety

1. Mindfulness Meditation
- **Practice Mindfulness:** Engage in mindfulness meditation by anchoring your attention to the present moment with an attitude of openness and non-judgment. This practice might include focusing on the rhythm of your breathing, the subtle sensations in various parts of your body, or the ebb and flow of your thoughts and emotions. The key is to observe these experiences with gentle curiosity rather than trying to alter or judge them.
- **Structured Mindfulness Exercises:** Incorporate structured mindfulness exercises into your routine, such as guided meditations, which can be particularly helpful for beginners. These guided sessions can provide direction and focus, helping you to stay anchored in the practice.
- **Benefits:** Mindfulness meditation has been shown to reduce the tendency to engage in rumination—the repetitive looping of thoughts, often negative, that can

escalate stress and anxiety. Furthermore, mindfulness enhances emotional regulation, the skill of managing and responding to our emotional landscape with greater mastery, leading to improved mood and decreased anxiety levels.

- **Integration into Daily Life:** To maximize the benefits, integrate mindfulness practices into your daily activities. This could mean being fully present and attentive during routine tasks like eating, showering, or walking. Such integration can help mitigate the continuous stream of stressors characteristic of modern life, fostering a sense of calm and centeredness.

- **Regular Practice:** Consistency is critical when it comes to mindfulness. Aim to practice daily, even if it's only for a few minutes at a time. As mindfulness becomes a habit, you may find that your general level of stress and anxiety decreases, and your ability to cope with challenging situations improves.

By embracing mindfulness and incorporating it into your life, you can develop a more tranquil mind and a more resilient response to the stress and anxiety that are often inherent in our fast-paced world. Remember, managing stress and anxiety is not about eliminating these feelings entirely but about cultivating the tools and mindset to navigate them effectively.

2. Deep Breathing Exercises

Deep breathing exercises are a practical, accessible tool for mitigating stress and anxiety, with the added advantage of being able to be practiced almost anywhere and at any time.

- **Diaphragmatic Breathing:** This technique involves a conscious shift from shallow, chest breathing to deeper, more fulfilling breaths initiated from the diaphragm. To practice diaphragmatic breathing, find a comfortable seated or lying position and place one hand on your belly. As you inhale slowly and deeply through the nose, focus on making the hand on your belly rise, rather than your chest, indicating that the diaphragm is pulling air into the base of your lungs. Then, exhale gently, either through the nose or mouth, feeling the belly fall. This method encourages full oxygen exchange and has a calming effect on the body's physiological stress response.

- **Benefits of Diaphragmatic Breathing:** Regular practice of diaphragmatic breathing can lead to a reduction in the body's "fight-or-flight" stress hormones, an increase in the relaxation response, and a host of related benefits, such as lower heart rate, reduced blood pressure, and a feeling of calm and centeredness.

- **4-7-8 Technique:** Developed as a relaxation exercise, the 4-7-8 technique is a simple yet effective way to help control anxiety and promote better sleep. The pattern of breathing this technique prescribes maximizes the amount of oxygen that fills the lungs, encouraging a slowing down of the heart rate and promoting a state of calm throughout the body. To practice, fully exhale through your mouth, then close it and inhale quietly through your nose to a mental count of four. Hold your breath for a count of seven, then exhale completely through your mouth, making a whoosh sound, to a count of eight. This one breath cycle can be repeated three to four times.

- **Application of Deep Breathing:** Deep breathing exercises like the 4-7-8 technique can be especially useful during moments of acute stress or when preparing for a situation that you anticipate will be anxiety-provoking. By integrating these practices into your daily routine, they can serve as a preventative measure, helping to maintain a state of relaxation and preventing the build-up of stress throughout the day.

Incorporating deep breathing techniques into your stress management arsenal can significantly shift your body's response to stress, transitioning from a heightened state of anxiety to a more relaxed, controlled state of being. With habitual practice, these breathing techniques can become second nature, providing you with a readily available tool to combat stress and anxiety whenever they arise.

3. Progressive Muscle Relaxation (PMR)

Progressive Muscle Relaxation (PMR) is a technique designed to reduce stress and anxiety through a two-step process of tensing and then relaxing the muscles. By deliberately working through various groups of muscles, you can develop a deeper awareness of physical tension and learn to control the relaxation response.

- **Tense and Relax Technique:** Begin by finding a quiet and comfortable place where you can sit or lie down without interruption. Starting at one end of your body, such as the feet, purposefully tense the muscles for approximately five seconds, then release them abruptly, relaxing for 20 to 30 seconds. It's important to focus intently on the sensation of release as the muscles let go of the tension. This intentional contraction followed by relaxation helps to differentiate the feelings associated with each state, training your body to recognize and enter a state of relaxation more easily.
- **Progress Through Muscle Groups:** Methodically move through the body, targeting one muscle group at a time. After the feet, move to the calves, thighs, glutes, and so on, working your way up to the facial muscles. Ensure you cover all major muscle groups, giving attention to both sides of the body equally.
- **Benefits of PMR:** As you practice PMR, you'll likely begin to notice a reduction in the day-to-day tension you carry in your body. This technique is not only effective for easing the physical symptoms of stress but can also enhance mental relaxation. As the body relaxes, the mind often follows, leading to decreased levels of mental stress and anxiety.
- **Routine Practice:** Incorporating PMR into your daily routine can enhance its benefits. With regular practice, your body becomes more adept at entering a relaxed state

on cue, and you develop a heightened awareness of when you're holding tension. Over time, this practice can contribute to a significant reduction in your overall stress levels and an increased sense of physical and emotional well-being.

- **Incorporate Breathing:** To deepen the relaxation experience, combine PMR with deep breathing exercises. As you release tension from each muscle group, complement the release with a slow and deliberate exhale, further enhancing the sense of relaxation.
- **Application in Stressful Situations:** Once you become proficient in PMR, you can use this technique in situations where you feel increased stress or impending anxiety. Even without going through the full routine, simply tensing and then relaxing your shoulders, neck, or any other area where you typically hold stress can provide immediate relief.

PMR can be a particularly effective technique for those who experience stress in a very physical way. By learning to control the physical manifestation of stress through muscle relaxation, the mind-body connection is strengthened, contributing to improved management of stress and anxiety in daily life.

4.Regular Physical Activity
Incorporating regular physical activity into your lifestyle is a well-documented strategy for alleviating stress and bolstering mental health. The benefits of exercise extend far beyond the physical realm, influencing mood and cognitive function due to its impact on various chemicals in the brain.

- **Exercise as a Stress Reliever:** Engage in physical activities that you enjoy and that fit your current level of fitness and lifestyle. The range of activities that can reduce stress is vast, from the steady rhythmic pace of walking or swimming, which can create a meditative effect, to the focused movements of yoga that combine physical exertion with mindful breathing. Even high-energy activities like weightlifting or interval training can serve as powerful stress relievers by channeling and dissipating tension.

- **Endorphin Release:** Physical activity stimulates the production of endorphins, the body's natural mood elevators. This release can lead to an improvement in mood, a phenomenon often referred to as the "runner's high." However, it's not limited to running; any form of exercise can result in this beneficial boost.
- **Reduction of Stress Hormones:** Regular exercise helps regulate and lower the body's stress hormones, such as cortisol, over time. By contributing to a balanced endocrine system, exercise can temper the physiological responses to stress, helping your body to react more calmly in stressful situations.
- **Consistency is Key:** Establish a regular exercise routine by aiming for at least 3o minutes of moderate exercise on most days of the week. Consistency in your exercise regimen helps maintain the stress-reducing benefits over the long term. If 3o minutes at once seems daunting, consider breaking it down into smaller, more manageable chunks of time, such as three 1o-minute walks throughout the day.
- **Build a Routine:** Making exercise a regular part of your daily schedule can enhance its effectiveness as a stress management tool. Whether it's a morning jog to start the day, a cycle after work to decompress, or a yoga session to relax in the evening, having a set routine can help ensure that exercise is a consistent part of your life.
- **Physical Activity as a Ritual:** Beyond the biological impacts, the ritual of exercise can provide a sense of predictability and control that counterbalances the chaotic nature of stress. The routine can become a sanctuary of time that is solely yours, free from the demands and anxieties of everyday life.

By integrating regular physical activity into your life, you're not only fostering a healthier body but also cultivating a more resilient mind. The consistency of this practice lays the groundwork for a robust defense against the adverse effects of stress and anxiety, and with time, can significantly enhance your overall quality of life.

5. Adequate Sleep

Adequate sleep is a cornerstone of stress management and overall health. Quality sleep acts as a reset for the brain and body, allowing for emotional and physical recuperation. Implementing good sleep hygiene practices can profoundly impact your ability to handle stress and maintain equilibrium.

- **Sleep Hygiene Practices:** Establishing a consistent sleep schedule by going to bed and waking up at the same time every day helps set your body's internal clock. Create a restful sleeping environment that is dark, quiet, and cool, and invest in a comfortable mattress and pillows. Be mindful of your exposure to screens and bright lights in the evening, as these can disrupt your natural circadian rhythms.
- **Pre-Sleep Routine:** Develop a pre-sleep routine that signals to your body it's time to wind down. This might include reading, taking a warm bath, or engaging in gentle stretches or relaxation exercises. Dimming the lights and engaging in calm activities can assist in the transition to sleep.
- **Avoid Stimulants:** Be cautious with the consumption of stimulants such as caffeine and nicotine, especially in the hours leading up to bedtime. Similarly, while alcohol might initially make you feel drowsy, it can disrupt your sleep cycle once you're asleep.
- **Relaxation Techniques:** Techniques such as progressive muscle relaxation, deep breathing, or visualization can be particularly effective when used as part of your bedtime routine. They help to calm the mind and reduce the physical tension that can interfere with sleep. Apps or

audio recordings that guide you through these processes can be helpful tools.

- **Mindfulness and Meditation:** Mindfulness meditation can also be a valuable practice before bed. By focusing on the present and observing thoughts without judgment, you can break the cycle of stress-induced rumination that often hinders sleep.
- **Napping Wisely:** If you need to make up for lost sleep, a short nap can help improve mood, alertness, and performance. However, limit naps to 20-30 minutes in the early afternoon to avoid disrupting your nighttime sleep.
- **Address Sleep Disorders:** If you suspect that you have a sleep disorder such as insomnia or sleep apnea, seek medical advice. These conditions can significantly impact your health and quality of life, including your ability to manage stress.

Ensuring adequate sleep is a form of self-respect and an acknowledgment of the body's need for restoration. By prioritizing good sleep hygiene and using relaxation techniques to improve sleep quality, you empower yourself to face the challenges of the day with renewed energy and resilience.

6. Healthy Eating Habits

What we consume has a direct impact on our body's stress response system. A balanced diet not only nourishes the body but also stabilizes mood and energy levels, providing a strong physiological foundation for combating stress and anxiety.

- **Balanced Diet:** Strive for a diet that includes a wide variety of foods, ensuring you receive a comprehensive range of nutrients that support overall health and well-being. Incorporate plenty of fruits and vegetables, which are high in vitamins, minerals, and antioxidants— nutrients that are essential for brain health and can mitigate the impact of stress on the body. Lean proteins provide the amino acids necessary for neurotransmitter function, which in turn can influence mood and stress responses. Whole grains offer a steady supply of energy, preventing the blood sugar spikes and crashes that can exacerbate feelings of stress and anxiety.

- **Mindful Eating:** Adopt a mindful approach to eating by paying attention to the flavors, textures, and sensations of your food. Mindful eating can promote a more gratifying and less stressful experience with meals, encouraging you to slow down and enjoy your food without overeating.
- **Limit Stimulants:** Be aware of your intake of substances that can increase anxiety, such as caffeine and sugar. While they may offer a temporary boost in energy, they can also lead to jitteriness, heightened anxiety, and disrupted sleep patterns. If you consume caffeinated beverages, try to do so earlier in the day and in moderation.
- **Stay Hydrated:** Adequate hydration is crucial for maintaining cognitive function and managing stress. Even mild dehydration can affect mood, concentration, and energy levels. Aim to drink plenty of water throughout the day, and consider other sources of hydration like herbal teas or infused water with fruits.
- **Regular Meals and Snacks:** Eating regular meals and snacks prevents dips in blood sugar levels that can lead to irritability and increased stress. Planning meals and snacks can ensure you have healthy options on hand, reducing the temptation to reach for sugary or fatty comfort foods during times of stress.
- **Nutritional Support for Stress:** Certain nutrients, such as magnesium, omega-3 fatty acids, and B vitamins, have been shown to support the body's stress response. Including foods rich in these nutrients, like leafy greens, fatty fish, and nuts, can help bolster your resilience to stress.

A diet that supports your physical health can also support your mental health, creating a virtuous cycle that enhances your capacity to manage stress and anxiety. Remember, establishing healthy eating habits doesn't require perfection. Instead, aim for consistency and balance, making choices that support both your physical health and emotional well-being.

Daily Adaptation and Application of Relaxation and Mindfulness Techniques

Integrating Mindfulness into Daily Life

Once learned, mindfulness offers a range of benefits if systematically integrated into daily activities. It extends beyond isolated meditation moments to every part of the day. For example, you can practice mindfulness while engaging in activities such as eating, driving, or during work breaks. This constant attention can transform routine activities into moments of calm and reflection, helping you maintain a lower stress level throughout the day.

Implementing Breathing Techniques

Incorporating deep breathing into your routine can serve as a powerful immediate calming tool. It's advisable to establish specific times during the day, perhaps before stressful tasks or important meetings, to dedicate to short sessions of diaphragmatic breathing or the 4-7-8 technique. This not only prepares you to better handle impending stress but also reinforces the habit of using breathing as a regular self-management tool.

Regular Practice of Progressive Muscle Relaxation

Progressive Muscle Relaxation (PMR) is particularly effective when incorporated into your evening routine. Regularly practicing PMR can significantly reduce the levels of physical and mental stress accumulated throughout the day. Consider dedicating time to PMR before bedtime to improve sleep quality and to develop greater awareness of tension areas in your body, facilitating deeper and more conscious relaxation.

Creating a Personal Routine

Developing a personalized routine that incorporates these techniques can transform how you handle stress. Determine which practices work best for you and adapt them to your lifestyle. For example, you might find that morning meditation positively prepares you for the day, or that some deep breathing sessions in the afternoon reinvigorate you for the remaining challenges.

Responding to Stressful Situations

Once these practices become an integral part of your routine, you can actively use them as immediate responses to stressful situations. If you find yourself in a suddenly stressful situation, take a moment to quickly apply a deep breathing technique or a brief mindfulness exercise. This can not only mitigate your stress response in real-time but can also prevent the escalation of anxiety.

Monitoring and Adjusting

It is crucial to monitor the effectiveness of the techniques over time and adjust them as necessary. Some techniques may be more effective than others depending on the circumstances or may become less effective if the routine becomes too mechanical. Maintain a flexible approach and be open to adjusting practices to ensure they remain effective and relevant to your current needs.

Adopting these techniques in the context of your daily life not only improves stress and anxiety management but also enhances your quality of life, providing you with tools to better handle daily challenges and to live with greater presence and calm.

CHAPTER 7
CULTIVATING SELF-ESTEEM AND CONFIDENCE

Understanding Self-Esteem

Self-esteem is more than just feeling good about oneself; it's a fundamental component of personal development and emotional health. It influences how individuals face challenges, interact with others, and pursue their goals. Healthy self-esteem acts as an anchor that keeps individuals steady in turbulent times, fostering resilience and a proactive approach to life.

Definition and Importance

Self-esteem is essentially how much we value ourselves. It's our internal sense of worth that influences our belief in our abilities, our right to be happy, and what we deserve from life. This core component of emotional health is crucial because it dictates how people treat us, how we interact with others, and how we cope with challenges. High self-esteem isn't just about feeling good — it's about recognizing your inherent value and possessing a stable sense of self-worth regardless of external circumstances.

Healthy self-esteem enables individuals to make confident, informed decisions, engage in mutually respectful relationships, and persist in the face of adversity toward achieving their goals. Conversely, low self-esteem can lead to poor decision-making, toxic relationships, and a general reluctance to pursue one's aspirations.

Factors Influencing Self-Esteem

Self-esteem is shaped by a multitude of factors throughout our lives, each playing a crucial role in developing how we perceive and value ourselves:

- **Childhood Experiences:** The environment in which we grow up has a profound impact on our self-esteem. Positive interactions with parents, teachers, and peers, characterized by encouragement and praise, can foster a robust sense of self-worth. Conversely, experiences of criticism, neglect, or abuse can severely diminish our self-esteem. Early experiences can set the foundation for our self-image and influence our confidence as we navigate through later stages of life.

- **Social Comparisons:** With the rise of social media, it has become increasingly common to compare oneself to others. These comparisons often involve idealized portrayals that can distort our self-view and negatively impact our self-esteem. It's crucial to recognize and mitigate the effects of such comparisons, as they can lead to feelings of inadequacy and dissatisfaction with one's own achievements and appearance.

- **Successes and Failures:** Our achievements and setbacks significantly influence our self-esteem. Successes, especially when they align with our goals and values, can greatly enhance our self-esteem by affirming our abilities and increasing our confidence. Conversely, repeated failures might lead to a diminished self-view, particularly if these failures are internalized as a reflection of personal worth. It's important to view failures as opportunities for learning and growth rather than as reflections of inherent incapacity.

- **Criticism and Self-Talk:** The way we process criticism and engage in self-talk plays a critical role in shaping our self-esteem. Constructive criticism can be a powerful tool for personal growth if it is interpreted correctly and incorporated into our self-improvement strategies. However, if criticism leads to negative self-talk, it can be damaging to our self-esteem. Cultivating a habit of positive self-talk can reinforce self-worth and resilience, whereas negative self-talk can perpetuate self-doubt and diminish self-esteem.

Understanding and addressing these influential factors are essential for nurturing a healthy self-esteem. By actively recognizing and modifying the influences shaping our self-perception, we can enhance our self-esteem and, consequently, improve our overall life satisfaction and effectiveness in achieving personal and professional goals. This foundational self-awareness allows us to build a life that not only feels fulfilling but also empowers us to navigate challenges with confidence and resilience.

Building Confidence

Overcoming Self-Doubt

Self-doubt can be a significant barrier to achieving one's potential, often manifesting as an internal critic that questions one's abilities and worth. To build confidence, it's crucial to address and overcome these doubts:

- **Cognitive-Behavioral Techniques:** These involve identifying and challenging the automatic negative thoughts that underpin self-doubt. By questioning the evidence for these thoughts, considering alternative interpretations, and testing out new beliefs in real-life actions, individuals can shift their mindset from one of doubt to one of possibility and capability.

- **Practical Exercises for Taking Small Risks:** Confidence grows with experience. Taking on small challenges that are slightly out of one's comfort zone can significantly boost self-belief. Each small success builds a foundation for greater achievements, reinforcing the belief in one's ability to succeed.

- **Mindfulness:** Mindfulness meditation helps individuals observe their thoughts without judgment. Regular practice enables people to detach from negative self-talk and understand that thoughts are not facts, thereby reducing the impact of self-doubt on their emotional state.

Use of Affirmations

Affirmations are positive, empowering statements that can reprogram the mind to believe in one's capabilities and worth. They are most effective when they are personalized, positively framed, and repeated regularly:

- **Creating Effective Affirmations:** The best affirmations are those that resonate personally, are stated in the present tense, and focus on positive attributes and goals. For instance, "I am confident and competent in my work," rather than, "I will no longer feel incompetent."

- **How and When to Use Them:** Affirmations are most effective when repeated regularly, particularly at the start of the day or during challenging times. They can be written down and posted in visible locations, recited during meditation, or repeated mentally during stressful situations.

- **Making Affirmations Powerful:** Consistency is key in making affirmations work. Combining affirmations with visualization techniques, where you imagine yourself successfully handling a situation or achieving a goal, can enhance their effectiveness and impact on self-esteem.

Success Stories

Inspirational stories of individuals who have successfully enhanced their self-esteem and confidence can serve as powerful motivators. These narratives often highlight:

- **The Strategies Used:** Whether it's taking up new challenges, using affirmations, or engaging in community activities, these stories demonstrate practical steps taken by individuals to improve their self-esteem.

- **The Benefits Gained:** Success stories typically showcase how increased confidence has led to better relationships, career advancement, and a more fulfilling life, providing readers with tangible examples of the value of investing in their self-confidence.

CHAPTER 8
ENHANCING SELF-AWARENESS

Self-awareness stands as a foundational element of emotional intelligence, playing a pivotal role in both personal development and professional success. This comprehensive understanding of one's internal states, preferences, resources, and intuitions not only enhances personal growth but also improves interactions in various aspects of life.

- **Definition and Relevance:** Self-awareness involves a deep understanding of your emotions, behaviors, strengths, and weaknesses. It enables an individual to recognize their emotional triggers, align their actions with their values, and understand their impact on others. In professional settings, self-awareness contributes to more effective leadership, decision-making, and conflict resolution. It empowers individuals to manage their reactions and adapt their behaviors to different situations, which is crucial for navigating the complexities of workplace dynamics and personal relationships.

Components of Self-Awareness:

- **Internal Self-Awareness:** This aspect focuses on understanding one's own values, desires, thoughts, and emotions. It allows individuals to make decisions that are more aligned with their true selves, leading to greater satisfaction and effectiveness in their actions. Techniques such as mindfulness meditation, reflective journaling, and introspection are valuable for cultivating internal self-awareness. By regularly engaging in these practices, individuals can develop a clearer sense of their motivations and the emotional landscapes that influence their behavior.

- **External Self-Awareness:** Understanding how others perceive us is equally important. This form of self-awareness helps individuals gauge the effectiveness of their social interactions and adjust their behaviors accordingly. It can be enhanced through feedback from peers, mentors, and even through observing others' reactions to one's behaviors. External self-awareness is crucial for developing empathy and improving communication skills, both of which are essential for successful interpersonal engagements.

By nurturing both internal and external self-awareness, individuals can achieve a well-rounded self-perception that fosters greater control over their actions and reactions. This dual perspective not only enhances one's ability to navigate personal challenges but also amplifies efficacy in professional roles, particularly in leadership and collaborative environments. As individuals become more attuned to their inner drivers and the perceptions of others, they unlock the potential to transform both their personal lives and career trajectories profoundly.

Developing and Applying Self-Awareness
Self-awareness is an indispensable skill that enhances decision-making, relationship management, and personal growth. It involves a deep understanding of one's emotions, strengths, weaknesses, and behaviors and how these impact interactions with others and personal choices. This section expands on practical strategies to enhance both internal and external self-awareness, demonstrating how these strategies can be applied effectively in daily life.

Enhancing Internal Self-Awareness:

- **Mindfulness and Reflection:** Engaging in mindfulness practices such as meditation, and reflective journaling can profoundly deepen one's understanding of personal motivations and emotional responses. Regular mindfulness meditation helps in observing one's thoughts and feelings without judgment, fostering a deeper connection with the inner self. Reflective journaling serves as a tool to document daily experiences and emotional responses, which can reveal patterns and triggers in behavior, offering valuable insights for personal development.

- **Feedback Loops:** Creating and maintaining effective feedback loops with trusted peers, mentors, or coaches is crucial for identifying personal blind spots and areas requiring improvement. This feedback, when received and processed constructively, can lead to significant personal growth and enhance one's self-awareness. It is important to approach feedback with openness and the willingness to change, which are essential for true self-improvement.

Enhancing External Self-Awareness:

- **Social Perception:** Developing techniques such as empathetic listening and perspective-taking enhances one's ability to understand how others perceive them. This awareness is crucial for adjusting behaviors and improving communication styles to foster better personal and professional relationships.

- **Role of Body Language:** Non-verbal cues, including body language, significantly influence how others perceive us. Being aware of and adjusting one's body language can improve the clarity and effectiveness of interpersonal communications. Training oneself to maintain eye contact, use open gestures, and adopt an attentive posture can convey confidence and respect for others, which are pivotal in successful interactions.

Practical Applications of Self-Awareness:
Self-awareness is not just a personal trait but a practical tool that can be applied to various aspects of life, enhancing decision-making, improving relationships, and fostering personal growth. Here's how enhanced self-awareness can be transformative:

In Decision Making:

- **Alignment with Core Values:** Understanding one's core values and emotional responses leads to more informed and consistent decision-making. With heightened self-awareness, individuals can make choices that truly reflect their personal and professional aspirations, which contributes to greater satisfaction and success in achieving goals.

- **Risk Assessment and Management:** Self-aware individuals are better equipped to assess risks and anticipate the emotional and practical impacts of their decisions. This can lead to more strategic thinking and less impulsive decision-making, especially in high-stakes environments.

In Relationship Management:

- **Enhanced Communication:** Knowing oneself deeply aids in expressing thoughts and emotions more clearly and understanding the emotional states of others. This can dramatically improve the quality of both personal and professional relationships by reducing misunderstandings and fostering empathy.

- **Conflict Resolution:** Self-awareness allows individuals to recognize their contribution to conflicts and better understand the perspectives of others. This awareness is crucial in resolving disputes amicably and building stronger, more resilient relationships.

In Personal Development:

- **Targeted Growth:** By recognizing their strengths and weaknesses, individuals can design personal development plans that focus precisely on areas that need improvement or further development. This targeted approach makes the process of personal growth more efficient and rewarding.

- **Adaptability and Learning:** Self-aware individuals are more adaptable and open to learning, as they are aware of their learning styles, emotional triggers, and limitations. This openness is essential in today's rapidly changing world, where continuous learning is key to personal and professional success.

By integrating self-awareness into everyday life, individuals can enhance their decision-making abilities, improve their relationships, and accelerate their personal development. This chapter not only aims to outline the benefits and applications of self-awareness but also to provide readers with actionable strategies to cultivate a deeper, more reflective understanding of themselves. Such self-awareness is essential for anyone seeking to live a more fulfilled, productive, and authentic life.

CHAPTER 9
HARNESSING PERSONAL STRENGTHS

Identifying Personal Strengths:

Understanding and leveraging personal strengths is essential for achieving success and fulfillment in both personal and professional life. This section delves into effective methods for recognizing and articulating individual strengths, providing practical tools and strategies for self-discovery and application.

Methods for Identifying Strengths:

- **Self-Assessment Exercises**: Explore a variety of approaches to help you identify your strengths. This could involve reflecting on what you naturally do well or situations in which you feel most competent and engaged.

- **Feedback Analysis**: I encourage you to actively seek feedback from colleagues, mentors, and supervisors. This feedback can be invaluable in identifying strengths that are recognized and valued by others.

- **Personal Reflection Exercises**: I will guide you through structured reflection exercises designed to help you analyze past successes and challenges. Reflecting on your personal experiences can illuminate recurring behavioral patterns and skills that signify underlying strengths.

Evaluating and Leveraging Strengths:

- **Contextual Evaluation**: Learn to assess the relevance and impact of your strengths in different situations. This involves understanding when and how a particular strength can be most effectively applied, whether in problem-solving, leading teams, or enhancing personal relationships.

- **Strategic Application**: Discuss strategies for leveraging your strengths in a way that maximizes their impact. This includes aligning strengths with career objectives, using them to overcome or compensate for weaknesses, and enhancing team dynamics by complementing the strengths of others.

- **Goal Alignment**: Emphasize the importance of aligning your strengths with personal and professional goals. Illustrate how this alignment can lead to greater job satisfaction, performance, and overall well-being.

By focusing on these techniques, you can gain a deeper understanding of your unique strengths and learn how to effectively harness them. This not only boosts your self-confidence but also enhances your ability to make significant contributions in your personal life and professional careers.

Using Strengths to Overcome Weaknesses

Explore strategies that enable individuals to utilize their strengths to mitigate and improve areas of weakness, ultimately leading to more comprehensive personal growth.

- **Strategies for Addressing Weaknesses:** Offer techniques for using strengths as a framework to improve weaker areas. For example, if someone excels in strategic thinking but struggles with detail-oriented tasks, they might use their strategic ability to develop systems that ensure finer details are managed.

- **Balancing Strengths and Weaknesses:** Discuss the balance between capitalizing on strengths and improving weaknesses, stressing the importance of focusing on strengths to drive personal and professional growth while managing weaknesses that could hinder progress.

- **Case Studies and Examples:** Provide real-life examples of how individuals have successfully identified their strengths and used them to compensate for or improve their weaker areas. These stories can inspire and illustrate practical applications of the concepts discussed.

Practical Applications:

- **In the Workplace:** Demonstrate how understanding and applying one's strengths can lead to better job performance, greater job satisfaction, and potential leadership opportunities.

- **In Personal Life:** Explore how personal strengths can enhance relationships, increase life satisfaction, and support personal hobbies and activities.

- **In Problem Solving and Innovation:** Show how individual strengths can be harnessed creatively to solve problems and innovate, whether in professional projects or personal challenges.

This chapter empowers readers to identify and utilize their strengths, enhancing their ability to overcome challenges and achieve their full potential. By understanding and applying their unique attributes, individuals can create fulfilling paths in both their personal and professional lives.

CHAPTER 10
SUSTAINING PERSONAL GROWTH

Maintaining Motivation and Momentum
Staying motivated and maintaining progress are crucial for anyone aiming to achieve long-term personal and professional goals. This section outlines effective strategies and practical tips for sustaining motivation and ensuring continual advancement toward your objectives.

Techniques for Sustaining Motivation:

- **Incremental Goals**: Set smaller, manageable milestones within larger goals to create a sense of progress and achievement. This technique helps maintain enthusiasm and commitment by providing frequent moments of success.

- **Celebrating Successes**: Emphasize the importance of recognizing and celebrating each success, no matter how small. Celebrations can reinforce positive behavior and boost morale, keeping the momentum going.

- **Motivational Tools**: Introduce motivational tools such as vision boards, which can visually represent your goals and dreams, or motivational quotes that inspire and uplift. These tools can serve as daily reminders of your aspirations and the reasons behind your hard work.

- **Understanding Motivation**: Dive into the psychological aspects of motivation, explaining theories like Self-Determination Theory, which emphasizes the roles of autonomy, competence, and relatedness in fostering intrinsic motivation.

Maintaining Progress:

- **Regular Reviews**: Encourage regular assessment of goals and progress to ensure they remain relevant and aligned with your personal growth and changes in circumstances. This could involve monthly or quarterly review sessions where goals are adjusted and refined as needed.

- **Resilience and Adaptability**: Highlight the importance of resilience in maintaining momentum. Learn how to develop a resilient mindset that helps you stay committed to your goals despite challenges and setbacks.

- **Accountability Partners**: Suggest the use of accountability partners or groups as a way to maintain motivation. Sharing goals with someone else can increase the likelihood of sticking to them because of the added pressure of external expectations.

- **Learning from Setbacks**: Emphasize learning from setbacks rather than being discouraged by them. View failures as opportunities to learn, grow, and refine your strategies.

By employing these strategies, you can keep your motivation high and your progress steady. This chapter aims to equip you with the tools you need to persistently pursue your goals, adapting and thriving in the face of both successes and challenges.

Embracing Lifelong Learning

In a rapidly changing world marked by technological advancements, the commitment to lifelong learning is more crucial than ever. This section highlights the undeniable benefits of continuous personal development and offers actionable strategies for integrating lifelong learning into daily life.

Importance of Lifelong Learning:

- **Enhancing Personal Efficacy:** Ongoing education and skill development are essential for maintaining personal efficacy in navigating both personal and professional challenges.

- **Adaptability in Changing Markets:** Continuous learning equips individuals with the flexibility to adapt to new technologies, industries, and job market demands, ensuring relevance and employability.

- **Success Stories:** Real-life examples from various fields demonstrate how lifelong learning has been pivotal for success and resilience.

Methods for Embracing Lifelong Learning:

- **Developing a Learning Plan:** Guide on how to create a comprehensive learning plan that includes formal education, informal learning opportunities, and hands-on experiences.

- **Leveraging Resources:** Diverse resources for learning, such as online courses, workshops, webinars, podcasts, and books, are recommended. Highlight how these resources can be utilized to pursue personal and professional interests.

- **Integrating Learning into Daily Routines:** Strategies to seamlessly integrate learning into daily life, such as listening to educational podcasts during commutes or dedicating time each week for online courses.

Practical Applications:

- **Career Advancement:** Illustrate how lifelong learning directly contributes to career advancement by keeping individuals competitive in their fields. Discuss the importance of upskilling and reskilling in response to industry trends.

- **Personal Enrichment:** Show how acquiring new skills or deepening knowledge in personal interest areas can lead to greater life satisfaction and personal fulfillment.

- **Adaptability and Innovation:** Emphasize how continuous learning fosters creativity and innovation, enabling individuals to proactively address challenges, adapt to change, and seize new opportunities.

This chapter aims to empower you with the tools and mindset necessary for embracing lifelong learning, thereby fostering ongoing growth and ensuring sustained success.

CONCLUSION
UNLOCKING YOUR FULL POTENTIAL

Reflecting on your journey of personal growth, it's essential to take a moment to appreciate how much you have learned and experienced. Each challenge you have faced and every milestone achieved represents a significant step on your path to realizing your full potential.

The importance of reflection cannot be overstated. Take the time to analyze past experiences, both successes and obstacles, as each contributes to your resilience and growth. Celebrating your successes is just as crucial; acknowledging your progress strengthens your self-esteem and motivates you to continue on your path.

Looking ahead, I encourage you to maintain the momentum of your personal development. **Set future goals** that reflect your personal values and long-term aspirations. These goals should challenge you and push you toward continual growth.

Stay committed to **ongoing self-improvement** and constantly seek new opportunities to learn and develop new skills. Embrace new challenges, as each new experience is a potential life lesson that can lead to significant and unexpected discoveries.

In conclusion, remember that the journey to realizing your full potential is a continuous path, filled with changes and growth. With dedication, adaptability, and resilience, you will always be able to navigate life's uncertainties while maintaining a clear sense of direction toward your goals.

Let the themes of this book inspire you, and use the tools and strategies you've learned to enhance every aspect of your life. It is your commitment and perseverance that will turn your aspirations into reality. You are the director of your personal story; make each chapter a testament to your growing ability and ongoing success.